# THE CREEK

## BY LIZ SONNEBORN

CONSULTANT: JOYCE BEAR
MANAGER, CULTURAL AND HISTORICAL PRESERVATION OFFICE
FOR THE MUSCOGEE (CREEK) NATION, OKMULGEE, OKLAHOMA

LERNER PUBLICATIONS COMPANY
MINNEAPOLIS

ABOUT THE COVER IMAGE: This leg rattle is made of turtle shells filled with pebbles. The Creek tie the rattles around their legs for ceremonial dances.

PHOTO ACKNOWLEDGMENTS:

The photos in this book are used with the permission of: Muscogee Creek Nation Communications Department, pp. 1, 3, 4, 14, 21, 32, 43, 46; © Marilyn "Angel" Wynn/Nativestock.com, pp. 5, 7, 8, 10, 11, 12, 13, 15, 16, 17, 19, 22, 23, 30, 31, 45, 47, 51; Research Division of the Oklahoma Historical Society, Twin Territories 21178_4_259, p. 9; Research Division of the Oklahoma Historical Society, Wright Collection, 14676, p. 18; Research Division of the Oklahoma Historical Society, Wright Collection, 14666, p. 20; Courtesy of Hargrett Rare Book & Manuscript Library/University of Georgia Libraries, p. 24; © North Wind Picture Archives, p. 25; British Museum, p. 26; Ohio Historical Society, p. 28; Museum of the City of Mobile, p. 29; Research Division of the Oklahoma Historical Society, McKenney Hall Collection, 20462_1_23, p. 33; Library of Congress, pp. 34 (LC-USZC4-7731), 37 (LC-USZC4-1756); © SuperStock, Inc./SuperStock, p. 35; Research Division of the Oklahoma Historical Society, OHS State Museum Murals, 6393, p. 36; Research Division of the Oklahoma Historical Society, McKenney Hall Collection, 20516_22, p. 38; Research Division of the Oklahoma Historical Society, Indians, 536, p. 39; Denver Public Library, Western History Collection, Standiford, J. F., X-30956, p. 40; Research Division of the Oklahoma Historical Society, Porter Collection, 3280, p. 41; Research Division of the Oklahoma Historical Society, Campbell Collection, 3905, p. 42; © Carlo Allegri/Getty Images, p. 48; © PandaAmerica.com. Coin design by Alex Shagin, p. 49; © Kit Howard Breen, p. 50.

Front Cover: © Marilyn "Angel" Wynn/Nativestock.com.

Lerner Publications Company
A division of Lerner Publishing Group
241 First Avenue North
Minneapolis, MN 55401 U.S.A.

Website address: www.lernerbooks.com


Library of Congress Cataloging-in-Publication Data

Sonneborn, Liz.
    The Creek / by Liz Sonneborn.
       p.    cm. — (Native American histories)
    Includes bibliographical references and index.
    ISBN-13: 978-0-8225-5913-9 (lib. bdg. : alk. paper)
    ISBN-10: 0-8225-5913-7 (lib. bdg. : alk. paper)
    1. Creek Indians—History. 2. Creek Indians—Social life and customs. I. Title. II. Series.
E99.C9S66 2007
975.004'97385—dc22                                            2005024303

Manufactured in the United States of America
1 2 3 4 5 6 – DP – 12 11 10 09 08 07

# CONTENTS

CHAPTER 1
FROM THE EARTH . . . . . . . . . . . . . . . . . . 4

CHAPTER 2
LIFE IN A CREEK TOWN . . . . . . . . . . 14

CHAPTER 3
DEALING WITH OUTSIDERS . . . . . . 21

CHAPTER 4
TO THE WEST . . . . . . . . . . . . . . . . . . . 32

CHAPTER 5
MODERN CREEK AND MUSCOGEE . . . 43

ACTIVITY . . . . . . . . . . . . . . . . . . . . . . . . 51

PLACES TO VISIT . . . . . . . . . . . . . . . . . 52

GLOSSARY . . . . . . . . . . . . . . . . . . . . . . 53

FURTHER READING . . . . . . . . . . . . . . . 54

WEBSITES . . . . . . . . . . . . . . . . . . . . . . 54

SELECTED BIBLIOGRAPHY . . . . . . . . . 55

INDEX . . . . . . . . . . . . . . . . . . . . . . . . . 56

# CHAPTER 1

# FROM THE EARTH

**LONG AGO, A GREAT CRACK IN THE EARTH** occurred somewhere in the West. People called the Cusseta crawled out of the crack and headed east. Eventually, they met another group of people, the Coweta. The Cusseta and the Coweta settled along rivers near one another.

This story was told by a Creek Indian leader named Chekilli in 1735. It explained how the two major towns of the Creek people came to be. The Creek were then the most powerful American Indian group in the southeastern United States.

Others knew the Creek as the relatives of the ancient people of the Mississippian cultures. The Mississippian people lived along the Mississippi and other river valleys in the Southeast. They left behind large earth mounds.

Hundreds of years ago, ancestors of the Creek people built huge earth temples. These mounds can still be seen at Ocmulgee National Monument, near Macon, Georgia.

The Creek Indians lived in dozens of towns scattered over their large homeland. It included most of present-day Georgia and Alabama and parts of Florida, Tennessee, and Louisiana.

## CREEK TOWNS

The Creek's homeland was covered with pine, oak, hickory, pecan, and other trees. Many streams and rivers flowed through these forests. The Creek people built their towns along the waterways.

## NAMING THE CREEK

No one knows for certain how the Creek people got their name. According to one explanation, they were first called the Creek in the 1700s. At that time, English traders often visited the American Indians living on the Ochese Creek (the modern-day Ocmulgee River). The Englishmen started referring to their trading partners as the Ochese Creek Indians. Over time, the name was shortened to the Creek.

The Creek built high walls around their towns
for protection. When a town became too big,
a new, smaller town was formed.

At the center of each town was the town
square. Here, people came together during the
summer months for meetings, dances, and other
religious ceremonies.

When it was cold, townspeople met inside a big
circular building called a *chakofa*. Its walls were
made of stacks of logs and clay, and its roof was
covered with bark. A large chakofa could hold as
many as five hundred people.

In the winter, the Creek built their homes out of mud, clay, grass, and tree branches.

Around the town square, families built their homes from clay and wood. Most families had two houses—one for summer and one for winter. Nearby, they built small structures for storing food.

## FAMILIES AND CLANS

Children, their parents, and their grandparents often lived together in the same house. After marriage, a husband moved into his wife's house. A man could marry more than one woman but only if his first wife approved.

Every Creek belonged to a clan. A clan is a group of people who came from the same ancient family. The Creek had about fifty clans. Many were named after animals, such as the Wolf clan and the Skunk clan. A man and woman could marry only if they were from different clans. Children always belonged to the clan of their mother.

Two young Creek women wearing traditional dress pose for a photo in 1902. Clan members of the same age treated one another as sisters and brothers.

The birth of a child was always a cause for celebration. The Creek especially welcomed twins. They believed that the younger twin was likely to grow up to become a gifted spiritual leader. Creek mothers and their female relatives raised the girls in the family. The uncles and other men on the mothers' side took care of the boys.

Chief Tomochichi sits with his nephew. Uncles on the mother's side teach their nephews skills, beliefs, and values that are important to the Creek people.

## A LAND OF PLENTY

Each family had its own garden. But families also shared a large field. It was farmed by everyone in their town. The Creek grew beans, squash, and melons. Their most important crop was corn.

The Creek roasted ears of corn in an open fire. Women also ground corn into flour and baked it into corn bread. Sometimes, they flavored the bread with wild berries and nuts. Plants were also gathered to make clothing. Women cooked, stored, and served food in baskets and clay pots.

Corn and squash are an important part of traditional Creek meals.

After the autumn harvest, Creek men went into the forest on hunting trips. All winter long, they tracked animals, large and small. Their favorite prey were deer and bears. These animals provided plenty of meat, and their skins and furs could be made into clothing. The Creek made an oil from bear fat. They rubbed the oil on their skin and hair to keep them moist.

Soft leather shoes called moccasins were made out of animal skins.

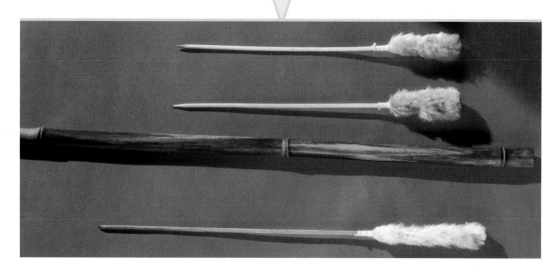

Creek men used blowgun darts to hunt small animals, such as squirrels, rabbits, ducks, and geese.

The Creek also added to their food supply by fishing. They caught trout, bass, catfish, eel, turtles, and perch using hooks, spears, traps, and bows and arrows. Sometimes, fishermen sprinkled a poisonous plant into the water. The poison stunned the fish, and they floated to the top of the water. Creek fishers scooped them up into fishing nets.

The Creek homeland had rich soil for farming and many natural resources. It provided the Creek with plenty of food and materials to make their houses and clothes. With some effort, the Creek could have everything they needed to lead a comfortable life.

# CHAPTER 2

# LIFE IN A CREEK TOWN

**EACH CREEK TOWN HAD A LEADER.** He was called a Mekko. The Mekko was assisted by a council of elders, known as the beloved men. A Mekko held his office only as long as the townspeople trusted him. He could be replaced if his followers became unhappy with his leadership.

Hopothle Mico was a leader of the Creek town of Tallassee, Georgia, in the late 1700s.

A Mekko had many duties. He was in charge of all activities in the town square. He managed the town's field, planned ceremonies, and solved disagreements. The Mekko also maintained the town's storehouse of food. He handed out food to the poor, making sure that no one in his town went hungry.

## WARS AND WARRIORS

The Mekko was also responsible for deciding when the town should go to war. The Creek usually sent out war parties in the spring.

Before going into battle, Creek warriors painted their faces and upper bodies with red and black paint. Their weapons included knives, clubs, bows and arrows, and shields. Men were eager to prove themselves in battle because a brave warrior was treated with respect.

While fighting their enemies, the Creek frequently took war captives. The townspeople would often allow captives to become members of the town. Male captives were not always so lucky. The women of the town usually tortured and killed them.

Early Creek warriors used clubs, blowguns, knives, and bows and arrows to fight their enemies. The Creek later added guns and metal weapons like this spear.

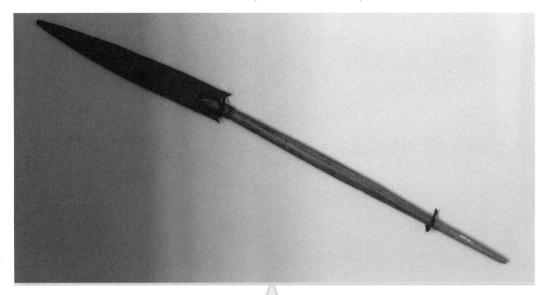

## HEALING THE SICK

The Creek held healers in high regard. Some healers had a special understanding of the spirit world. If someone was sick, these healers were called on to explain the cause of the illness.

Other healers were trained in treating diseases. They knew how to use more than one hundred different plants to make medicines. They prescribed other treatments as well. Some involved massaging or scratching patients or giving them special foods.

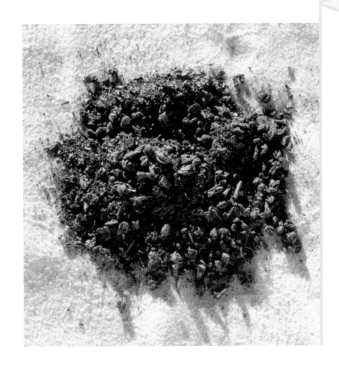

Creek healers treated people using a mixture of dried leaves and bark called kinnikinnick. It could be smoked, made into a drink, or rubbed on the body to cure sickness.

The Creek thought their healers could both cure and cause illness. As a result, when a patient died, his relatives sometimes blamed the doctor. Occasionally, they even tried to kill him in revenge.

## THE GREEN CORN CEREMONY

The Creek believed the world was full of spirits. To honor these spirits, the Creek performed ceremonies. The most important was the Green Corn Ceremony, or Posketv. The Creek held this ceremony at the end of the summer when the corn crop was ripe.

Creek women perform the Ribbon Dance during a Green Corn Ceremony in 1944.

The Green Corn Ceremony lasted several days. People came together to feast and play games. Many Creek danced, sang songs, and played music with drums and rattles. Men drank a tea called black drink to purify their bodies. Elders lectured the young people of their clan. The elders praised those who had behaved well over the last year and scolded those who had not.

With the Green Corn Ceremony, the Creek marked the beginning of a new year. They promised to forget old quarrels and forgive everyone for past crimes. The Creek believed the ceremony pleased the spirits. It also kept their own world in order.

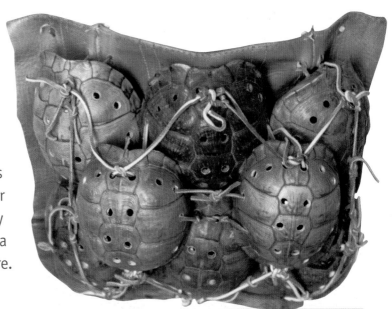

During the Green Corn Ceremony, Creek women wear turtle shell rattles around their legs as they dance around a sacred fire.

# PLAYING BALL

After the Green Corn Ceremony, the Creek of two rival towns came together to play a ball game. Teams of players used ball sticks to hurl a ball into a goal. The Creek took these ball games very seriously. Over the year, each team played many practice games so they would be well prepared. The games between towns often involved more than one hundred players. Big crowds gathered to watch, betting heavily on the results. The first team to score twenty goals won. As the losing team left the field, the winning team celebrated their victory by dancing around their goalpost.

The men and women in this photo are playing a friendly version of stickball. The goal is to hit the top of a pole with the ball.

# CHAPTER 3

# DEALING WITH OUTSIDERS

**IN 1539, AN ARMY OF SOLDIERS** marched into Creek territory. They were led by Hernando de Soto, an explorer from Spain. These Spaniards were the first non-Native Americans the Creek had ever encountered.

Hernando de Soto and his men landed in Florida in 1539. They brought with them many tools, weapons, and animals, such as horses, dogs, and pigs.

De Soto and his men did not make a good impression. As they stormed through the Southeast, they demanded food from the Creek and other American Indian tribes they met. To make sure the Creek did what they wanted, the Spaniards took some Creek leaders hostage.

Luckily for the Creek, de Soto's men did not stay long. However, they left behind germs that spread diseases, such as smallpox and measles. The Creek had not been exposed to these diseases before. Many people became very sick. Thousands died.

## THE CREEK CONFEDERACY

Over the next three hundred years, many other non-natives began to settle near Creek territory. Some were Spanish. Others were French. Still others were English.

In the past, Creek towns had been independent and their Mekkos had acted alone. But in the late 1600s and early 1700s, the Creek decided to band together to better protect their lands from outsiders. They formed a confederacy. Leaders from the towns gathered at a council to discuss problems that affected all Creek tribes.

In 1734, members of the Creek council and other tribes visited London. They met with British officials to make treaties.

The Creek, however, were living in different parts of the Southeast. The towns divided into two main groups. The Upper Creek lived in the mountains of northern and central Alabama. The Lower Creek lived close to the Atlantic coast and the Gulf of Mexico.

The Upper Creek lived along the Alabama, Coosa, and Tallapoosa rivers in Alabama. The Lower Creek lived along the Chattahoochee River in eastern Alabama and western Georgia.

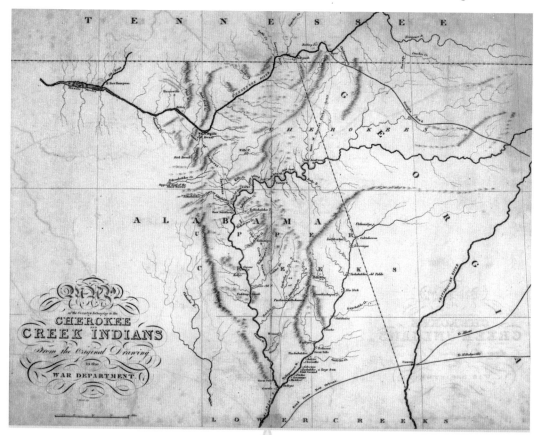

The Lower Creek's lands were close to Charles Town, a large English settlement in South Carolina. The Lower Creek often traded with the English there. The Creek gave the English deerskins and American Indian war captives, whom the English sold as slaves. In exchange, the Creek received guns, metal tools, and other goods made in England. These items made the Lower Creek more wealthy and powerful than the Upper Creek.

The Lower Creek traded with the English in Charles Town (Charleston), South Carolina. Some Lower Creek women married English traders.

In the 1730s, James Oglethorpe started the English colony of Georgia on Creek lands. The Creek helped protect Georgia against attacks.

## A NEW THREAT

In the mid-1770s, the English settlers declared their independence from Great Britain. Calling themselves Americans, they formed a new country, the United States. The Creek's territory was within its borders.

The United States presented a new and dangerous threat to the Creek. Many Creek leaders had signed treaties with Great Britain that allowed the English to live on Creek lands. Some Creek also helped defend English settlements against Spanish, French, and American attacks.

But when the settlements became part of the United States, so did much of Creek territory. American settlers seemed determined to take over the Creek's entire homeland. Under pressure, Creek leaders agreed to give up some land to the United States. But the Americans always wanted more.

**ALEXANDER MCGILLIVRAY** (ca. 1759–1793) was one of the most important Creek leaders of the 1700s. The son of a Creek woman and a Scottish trader, he tried to unite the Creek towns under his rule. On behalf of all the Creek people, McGillivray signed treaties with Spain and with the United States. He hoped these written agreements would keep the Spanish and the Americans out of Creek territory. However, at only thirty-four, McGillivray suddenly died of disease. With his early death, the dream of a completely united Creek people died as well.

In 1811, Tecumseh, a leader of the Shawnee tribe, visited the Creek. He was trying to persuade American Indians from many different tribes to rise up and fight the American settlers together. Tecumseh did not talk the Creek into joining his campaign. But he did convince some Upper Creek that it was time to go to war. The Lower Creek, though, did not want to fight. They still depended on the goods they received from American traders.

Tecumseh *(left)* met with American Indian tribes all across the eastern part of the United States.

## THE CREEK WAR

The pro-war Upper Creek were known as the Red Sticks. After several encounters with U.S. troops, they attacked Fort Mims in 1813. The Red Sticks killed hundreds of American soldiers and settlers and some Lower Creek hiding inside the fort.

The United States responded by sending a huge army to attack the Red Sticks. The army included thousands of men, led by General Andrew Jackson. The force was made up of U.S. soldiers and American Indian warriors, including some Lower Creek and Cherokees.

A warrior group of Upper Creek known as the Red Sticks attacked Fort Mims in 1813. Earlier that year, U.S. troops had raided Red Sticks who were returning from a trading trip.

The final battle of the Creek War was fought on March 27, 1814. The Red Sticks were camped along a bend of the Tallapoosa River, shaped like a horseshoe. Jackson's army sneaked up on the Red Sticks and launched a surprise attack. Within hours, about nine hundred Red Sticks were killed. After this victory, Jackson forced the Creek's leaders to sign the Treaty of Fort Jackson. In it, they agreed to give the United States nearly 23 million acres of land.

This drawing shows a battle between the Red Sticks and U.S. soldiers during the Creek War.

Red Stick leader William Weatherford *(right)* surrendered to Andrew Jackson *(left)* after the Battle of Horseshoe Bend.

The Creek War was a disaster for the Creek. Thousands were killed, and the survivors lost much of their territory in Georgia and Alabama. But perhaps worst of all, the war had pitted Creek against Creek, further dividing their people.

# CHAPTER 4

# TO THE WEST

**THROUGHOUT THE EARLY 1800S,**
the United States kept insisting that the Creek
give up more land to American settlers. The
members of the Creek Council wanted to
discourage its leaders from making deals with
U.S. officials. They declared that anyone who
did would be put to death.

William McIntosh, a leader of the Lower Creek, ignored the threat. In February 1825, he signed a treaty with the United States, selling Creek land in Georgia and Alabama. Three months later, Creek warriors surrounded his house. They shot and killed McIntosh when he tried to escape.

## GOING TO INDIAN TERRITORY

McIntosh's followers were no longer welcome among the Creek. His half brother, Rollie McIntosh, led them west. They ended up in an area called Indian Territory in present-day Oklahoma.

In 1825, William McIntosh and other Creek leaders were offered thousands of dollars to sign the illegal Treaty of Indian Springs.

In 1829, Andrew Jackson became president of the United States. Jackson wanted all the Creek to move to Indian Territory. American farmers were clamoring to take control of Creek lands. Most Creek did not want to go. Even as settlers started moving onto their lands, they refused to leave their homes.

Andrew Jackson *(left)* battled the Red Sticks in the Creek War. He became the seventh president of the United States in 1829.

In the 1830s, the Creek and other Native Americans were forced to move to Indian Territory in present-day Oklahoma.

In 1836, President Jackson sent the U.S. Army to round up the Creek and force them out. The army allowed a few Creek families who had been friendly to American settlers during the Creek War to stay in the Southeast. But everyone else was led west at gunpoint by soldiers.

Most Creek had to make the long trip to Indian Territory on foot. Others rode in wagons or on boats. U.S. soldiers captured and chained hundreds of Creek warriors who refused to go peacefully.

The very young and very old rode in wagons. Some traveled on steamboats for part of the trip. Everyone else made the trip on foot. During the long journey, the Creek were given little food or clothing. Many did not even have shoes. When winter set in, some people's feet became so frostbitten that they could not walk. Thousands died from hunger and disease. Their bodies were often tossed to the side of the road, where they were eaten by wild wolves.

# FIGHTING THE CIVIL WAR

The Creek's first years in Indian Territory were difficult. The land and weather were much drier and harsher in that part of the country. But slowly the Creek rebuilt their towns. Soon, though, the Creek were drawn into another bloody fight. It was called the American Civil War (1861–1865). In the United States, the states in the South and the North went to war. Both the North and the South wanted the Creek to join their sides.

The American Civil War divided the United States. More than 500,000 people died in battle or from disease.

Generally, the Upper Creek honored a treaty from 1832 and remained loyal to the U.S. government in the North. The Lower Creek decided to support the South. One group, led by Opothle Yoholo, wanted to stay out of the war altogether. To escape the fighting, he led thousands of followers north into Kansas. Hundreds died of starvation and in battle with a Southern force that included some Lower Creek warriors.

Opothle Yoholo led more than eight thousand Creek, Seminole, and Shawnee Indians to Kansas during the Civil War.

The American Civil War ended with a victory for the North. Although only some Lower Creek had sided with the South, the United States wanted to punish all the Creek. U.S. officials made the Creek sign a treaty with the U.S. government. The Creek had to give up half of their lands in Indian Territory.

## END OF A NATION

After the war, the Creek once again started rebuilding their nation. In 1867, they wrote a new constitution. It called for elections every four years to chose a principal chief. This leader would speak for the entire Creek Nation.

Samuel Checote was elected the first principal chief of the Creek Nation. He is pictured here outside his house.

Creek students at the Mission School in Muskogee Indian Territory, Oklahoma, pose for a picture. The girls are wearing European-style clothing and hairstyles.

In the late 1800s, more Creeks began to adopt the customs of European Americans. Many started speaking English and joined Christian churches.

But the biggest change in Creek life was the allotment policy. For centuries, the Creek had shared their lands with one another. U.S. officials, however, wanted to change this arrangement.

They insisted the Creek break up their land into small plots called allotments. Each family member would own an allotment.

Most Creeks did not want to divide their land. But U.S. officials ignored their wishes. By 1907, Creek territory was broken up into allotments. The Creek's lands in Indian Territory became part of the state of Oklahoma.

Pleasant Porter *(left)* represented the Creek Nation in the beginning of the 1900s.

**CHITTO HARJO** (1846–1909)
fought hard against the allotment
policy. When the Creek council
prepared to allot Creek land in the
early 1900s, Harjo and his
followers refused to accept their
allotments. They wanted the
U.S. government to honor its
original treaty. The treaty said
that Creek lands were owned by
all Creeks. Harjo soon had many
followers among the Creek and
other nearby tribes. In 1909, a few of
his followers had a shoot-out with local
lawmen. The police blamed Harjo. They shot him,
but he escaped into the southern part of Indian Territory,
where he died.

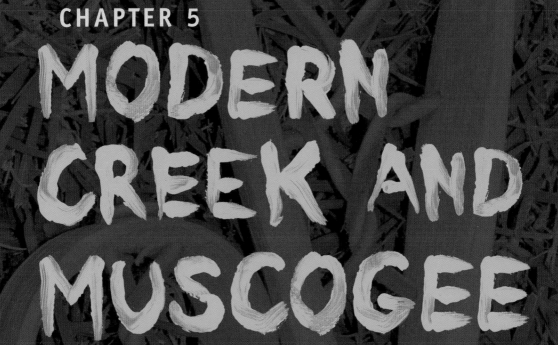

# CHAPTER 5

# MODERN CREEK AND MUSCOGEE

**THE EARLY 1900s WERE A HARD TIME FOR MANY CREEK PEOPLE.** Some had trouble making a living from their small plots of land. Others were cheated out of their land by con men.

## A DISCOVERY OF OIL

In the early 1900s, oil was discovered on some Creek allotments. This made a few Creek people wealthy. Officials in Oklahoma did not think these Creeks knew enough about U.S. culture to make business deals. They appointed non-American Indian guardians to take control of the business affairs of these oil-rich Creeks. Many of the guardians were dishonest, however. They stole oil money that rightfully belonged to Creek landowners. In one case, three small children were cheated out of their land and fortune after their parents died. Officials found them living in a hollow tree and searching the countryside for food.

Still, many Creek remained in Oklahoma. They lived in the towns the Creek built after moving west. In the 1950s and 1960s, the U.S. government encouraged Native Americans to leave their communities to find jobs. Some Creek moved to towns and cities throughout the United States. By 2000, seventy thousand people across the country said they were of Creek heritage.

# THE MUSCOGEE NATION

In the 1930s, a few Creek towns formed their own governments. The rest of the Creek in Oklahoma were represented by a principal chief chosen by the president of the United States. This changed in the 1970s, when the Creek and other Native American tribes were allowed to control their own governments again. For the first time in decades, the Creek were able to vote for their chief.

The Creek Council House in Okmulgee, Oklahoma, became the capital of the Creek Nation in 1878. It now serves as a museum and research center.

In 2006, members of the Muscogee (Creek), Chickasaw, Seminole, and Choctaw nations gathered to honor their people's role in building the state of Oklahoma during the last one hundred years. Chief A. D. Ellis of the Muscogee Nation is on the far left.

The Creek in the West call themselves the Muscogee (Creek) Nation. (Muscogee is the name of the language the Creek traditionally speak.) This American Indian tribe has about sixty-one thousand members.

In recent years, the government of the Muscogee Nation has worked hard to improve the lives of its people. It operates a hospital and health clinics that provide free health care for tribe members. The tribal government has also set up education programs for Creek children and adults. It has built homes for the elderly and provided food for those in need. The Muscogee Nation runs several businesses as well. They include a farm and a casino in Tulsa, Oklahoma.

The Creek Nation Travel Plaza in Okmulgee, Oklahoma, is open twenty-four hours a day.

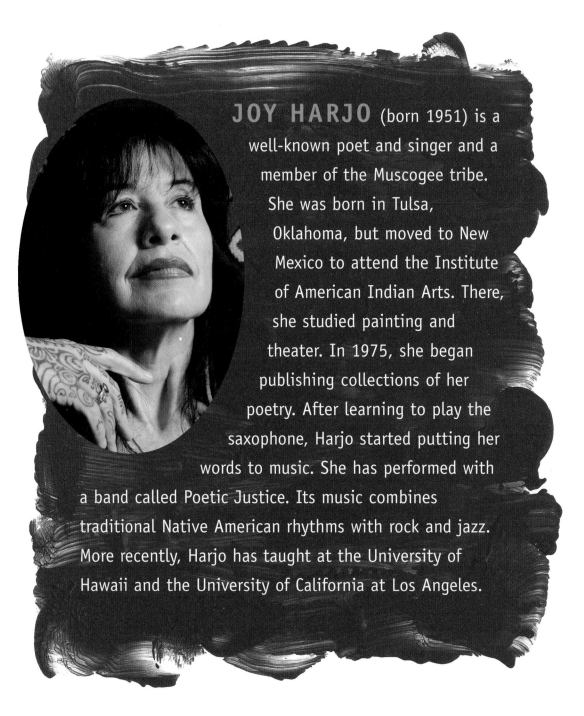

**JOY HARJO** (born 1951) is a well-known poet and singer and a member of the Muscogee tribe. She was born in Tulsa, Oklahoma, but moved to New Mexico to attend the Institute of American Indian Arts. There, she studied painting and theater. In 1975, she began publishing collections of her poetry. After learning to play the saxophone, Harjo started putting her words to music. She has performed with a band called Poetic Justice. Its music combines traditional Native American rhythms with rock and jazz. More recently, Harjo has taught at the University of Hawaii and the University of California at Los Angeles.

## THE POARCH BAND

A small group of Creek still live in the Southeast. They are known as the Poarch Band of Creek Indians. About one thousand Poarch Creek live in and near the town of Atmore, Alabama.

In 1984, the United States officially recognized the Poarch Band as an American Indian tribe. Since then, they have been given a small area of land, called a reservation. There, the tribe operates a bingo hall, motel, and restaurant.

This coin was made in 2004 to celebrate the Poarch Creek Indians' twenty years as a sovereign, or independent, nation. Members of the Poarch Band have worked hard to relearn their Muscogee language, culture, and traditions.

L. D. Thompson Sr. *(left)* and his son wear
Creek dance clothing at a powwow.

Wherever they live, the Creek are working hard
to preserve their old ways. Elders instruct children
in the Muscogee language. They also teach young
people to dance and play ball games just as the
Creek did centuries ago. And every summer, the
Creek come together in Oklahoma to hold the
Green Corn Ceremony. There, they celebrate the
past and present of the great Creek people.

# CREEK POTTERY

Traditionally, Creek women molded pots from clay they dug out of the ground. They did not decorate their pottery with paint. Instead, they pushed sticks and other objects into the wet clay to make patterns and shapes. Creek potters also carved designs into wooden paddles. They pressed the paddles into the clay to make complicated designs on the pots. Many Creek pots featured a band of decoration just under the rim.

You can make your own version of a decorated Creek pot with molding clay.

## WHAT YOU NEED:

*brown molding clay*
*stamps with geometric or*
*circular designs (see illustration)*

## WHAT TO DO:

1. Mold the clay into a small pot in a shape similar to the example pictured here.
2. Before the clay dries, press a stamp below the rim of the pot. Do this as many times as you need to create a patterned band all the way around the pot.
3. Let the pot dry.

# PLACES TO VISIT

### Creek Council House Museum
*Okmulgee, Oklahoma*
(918) 756-2324
The Creek Council House was built in 1878 in the Creek capital of Okmulgee. It was restored in the 1980s as a museum and research center devoted to the study of Creek history and culture.

### Five Civilized Tribes Museum
*Muskogee, Oklahoma*
(918) 683-1701
http://www.fivetribes.org
This museum was founded in 1966 to preserve the art, history, and culture of the Creek, Cherokee, Seminole, Chickasaw, and Choctaw Indians. The museum displays a large collection of traditional art and hosts yearly art competitions.

### Horseshoe Bend National Military Park
*Daviston, Alabama*
(256) 234-7111
http://www.nps.gov/hobe
Visitors to this national military park can tour the site of the Battle of Horseshoe Bend and learn about the battle, the Creek War, and the history of the southeastern United States.

### Muscogee (Creek) Nation
*Okmulgee, Oklahoma*
(800) 482-1979
http://www.muscogeenation-nsn.gov
The Muscogee Nation hosts several annual events, including art festivals and the Annual Creek Festival and Rodeo in June.

**Ocmulgee National Monument**
*Macon, Georgia*
(478) 752-8257
http://www.nps.gov/ocmu
The Ocmulgee National Monument features large land mounds built
by the ancestors of the Creek people during the Mississippian period.

# GLOSSARY

**allotment:** dividing large pieces of land into smaller pieces that are owned
by an individual or family. The small piece of land is called an
allotment.

**chakofa:** a winter meetinghouse in a Creek town

**clan:** a group of relatives within a tribe

**confederacy:** a group of peoples or nations that agree to work together as
a political unit

**constitution:** a set of laws adopted by a nation or group of people. The
laws state the rights of the people and the powers of the government.

**elder:** an older person

**Mekko:** the leader of a Creek town

**reservation:** an area of land set aside by the U.S. government for a
particular American Indian group

**treaty:** a written agreement between two or more nations or groups

**tribe:** a group of American Indians who share the same language,
customs, and religious beliefs

**united:** brought together for a common purpose

# FURTHER READING

Bruchac, Joseph. *The Great Ball Game: A Muskogee Story*. New York: Dial Books for Young Readers, 1994. The author retells the story of a ball game between the Birds and the Animals to decide which group is better.

Larrabee, Lisa. *Grandmother Five Baskets*. Tucson: Harbinger House, 1993. A young Creek woman learns how to make traditional baskets.

Scordato, Ellen. *The Creek Indians*. New York: Chelsea House Publishers, 1993. The author examines the life and culture of the Creek Indians.

Smith, Cynthia Leitich. *Jingle Dancer*. New York: Morrow Junior Books, 2000. In this modern-day story, a Muscogee girl tries to find tin jingles for the jingle dance dress she wants to wear at the next powwow. Back matter includes further information about Muscogee culture and a glossary.

Wilcox, Charlotte. *The Seminoles*. Minneapolis: Lerner Publications Company, 2007. This book describes the history and culture of the Seminole Indians, relatives of the Creek people who moved to Florida in the 1700s and 1800s.

# WEBSITES

**Muscogee (Creek) Nation**
http://www.muscogeenation-nsn.gov
This website provides information on the news, events, history, culture, economy, and government of the Muscogee (Creek) Nation in Okmulgee, Oklahoma.

**Poarch Creek Indians**
http://www.poarchcreekindians.org/
The government of the Poarch Band of Creek Indians operates from a 230-acre reservation in the town of Atmore, Alabama.

# SELECTED BIBLIOGRAPHY

Davis, Mary B., ed. *Native America in the Twentieth Century: An Encyclopedia.* New York: Garland Publishing, 1996.

Fogelson, Raymond D., ed. *Handbook of North American Indians: The Southeast.* Vol. 14. Washington, DC: Smithsonian Institution Press, 2004.

Green, Michael D. *The Creeks.* New York: Chelsea House Publishers, 1990.

Hoxie, Frederick E., ed. *Encyclopedia of North American Indians.* Boston: Houghton Mifflin, 1996.

Waldman, Carl. *Encyclopedia of Native American Tribes.* Rev. ed. New York: Facts on File, 1999.

# INDEX

allotment, 40–43
American Civil War, 37–39

ceremonies, 7, 15, 18–20, 50
Checote, Samuel, 39
clans, 8–9
clothing, 9, 11, 12, 40, 50
creation story, 4–5,
Creek War, 29–31, 34

de Soto, Hernando, 21–22
disease, 17, 22, 36

education and schools, 10, 17, 40,
    47, 50
explorers and settlers, 6, 21–23,
    25–29, 32, 34–35

family, 8–11, 41
farming, 11, 18, 47
fishing, 13
food, 8, 11–13, 15, 17, 19, 22

Green Corn Ceremony, 18–20, 50

Harjo, Chitto, 42
Harjo, Joy, 48
healers, 17–18
homeland, 5–6, 23, 24–26, 27, 31
homes, 8
Hopothle Mico, 15
hunting, 12, 13

Indian Territory, 33–37, 39, 40, 41, 42

Jackson, Andrew, 29–31, 34–35

language, 46, 49, 50
Lower Creek, 24–25, 28, 29, 33,
    38–39

McGillivray, Alexander, 27
McIntosh, William, 33
Mekkos, 14–15, 23
Mississippian cultures, 5
Muscogee (Creek) Nation, 46–47, 48

oil, 44
Opothle Yoholo, 38

Poarch Band of Creek Indians, 49
Porter, Pleasant, 41
pottery, 11, 51

stickball, 20

Tecumseh, 28
towns, 5–8, 11, 14, 15, 16, 20,
    23–24, 37, 44, 45
trade, 25, 28
treaties, 26–27, 30, 33, 38, 39, 42

Upper Creek, 24–25, 28–31, 38
U.S. soldiers, 29–30, 35–36

war and warriors, 15–16, 25, 26,
    28–31
Weatherford, William, 31